MW00803307

Studies and Melodious Etudes for Trombone

by Paul Tanner and Major Herman Vincent
in collaboration with James Ployhar

To The Teacher

"Studies And Melodious Etudes", Level III, is a supplementary technic book of the Belwin "STUDENT INSTRUMENTAL COURSE". Although planned as a companion and correlating book to the method, "The Trombone Student", it can also be used effectively with most intermediate or advanced trombone instruction books. It provides for extended and additional treatment in technical areas which are limited in the basic method because of lack of space. Emphasis is on developing musicianship through scales, warm-ups and technical drills, musicianship studies and interesting melody-like etudes.

The Belwin "STUDENT INSTRUMENTAL COURSE" - A course for individual and class instruction
of LIKE instruments, at three levels, for all band instruments.

EACH BOOK IS COMPLETE
IN ITSELF BUT ALL BOOKS
ARE CORRELATED
WITH EACH OTHER

METHOD
"The Trombone Student"
For Individual
or
Brass Class Instruction.

ALTHOUGH EACH BOOK CAN BE
USED SEPARATELY, IDEALLY,
ALL SUPPLEMENTARY BOOKS
SHOULD BE USED AS COMPANION
BOOKS WITH THE METHOD

STUDIES & MELODIOUS ETUDES

Supplementary scales, warm-up and technical drills, musicianship studies and melody - like etudes, all carefully correlated with the method.

TUNES FOR TECHNIC

Technical type melodies, variations, and "famous passages" from musical literature for the development of technical dexterity.

TROMBONE SOLOS

Four separate correlated solos, with piano accompaniment, written or arranged by Paul Tanner:
I Ain't Gonna Study War No
    More .... *Anonymous*
Nine Hundred Miles
    .... *Anonymous*
The Clarion.................... *Tanner*
Dawn is the Beginning..... *Tanner*

2

CORRELATED TROMBONE SOLOS

Four separate solos, with piano accompaniment, were written or arranged specifically for this course. We strongly encourage the use of these solos as supplementary lesson material.

I Ain't Gonna Study War No More
. . . . *arranged by Paul Tanner*

Nine Hundred Miles
. . . . *arranged by Paul Tanner*

The Clarion . . . . *Paul Tanner*

Dawn Is The Beginning . . . . *Paul Tanner*

SLIDE POSITION CHART

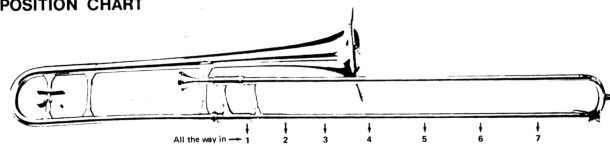

When two notes are shown together on the chart (F♯ and G♭), they have the same sound and are played on the same position.

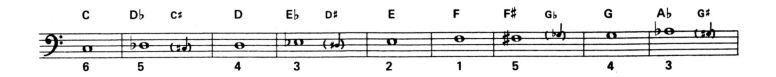

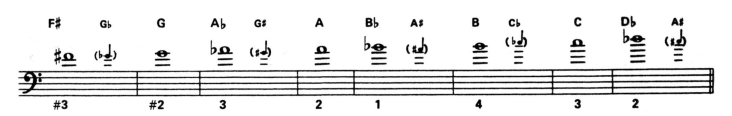

Position marked with a sharp are just a little shorter than normal, listen for correct intonation at all times.

© 1971 (Renewed 1999) Belwin Mills Publishing Corp. (ASCAP)
All Rights Assigned to and Controlled by Alfred Publishing Co., Inc.
All Rights Reserved including Public Performance. Printed in USA.

B.I.C.357

The Studies and Etudes on this page correlate approximately with Page 5, of the Trombone Method Book "The Trombone Student", Level Three, and the correlation is continued throughout the book.

Slowly - (Play with a steady tone)

Slowly - (Then work for speed)

Etude No. 1

SCHANTL

LIP SLURS

G MINOR SCALE STUDY

Etude No. 2

OCTAVE SLURS

Compare these two lines.   Play rhythms accurately.

Play the sixteenth notes very lightly.

RHYTHM STUDY

Compare the rhythms in measures 1 and 2.   Play them accurately.

Etude No. 3

KLOSE

Adagio

THIRDS AND ARPEGGIOS

Etude No. 4

LAURENT

Allegro

Fine

Vivo

D. C. al Fine

Work for speed.

LIP SLURS

TONGUING

Apply these rhythms to the scale above.   Work for speed.

Etude No. 5

Allegro

ARTICULATION

C MINOR SCALE STUDY

Etude No. 6

CONCONE

INTERVALS

Etude No. 7

BRANDT

LIP SLURS

(Also play 8va)

Also play:

etc.

$f \mathbin{>} p \ f \mathbin{>} p$ sim.

First, play with one flat in key signature, then with five flats (d minor and D♭ Major)
Sharp C in minor key only.

Etude No. 8

SCHANTL

Slowly

pp *ff* *pp* *ff* *sim.*

C MAJOR SCALE STUDY

Also play:

etc.

Repeat 3 times.

Etude No. 9

SMALL

Larghetto Expressivo

p

INTERVALS

Also play: etc.

Etude No. 10

SCHANTL

Allegro ma non troppo (not too fast)

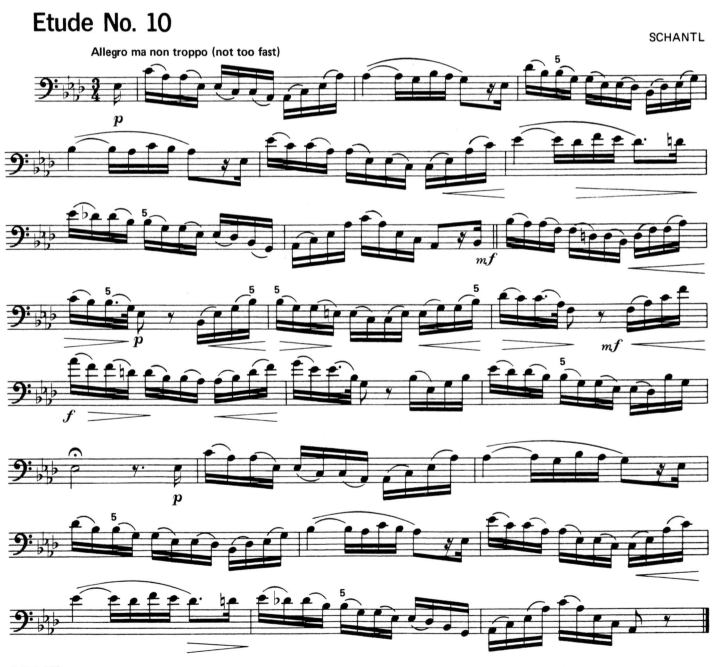

F MINOR SCALE STUDY

First, practice with four flats in the key signature then with one flat (f minor and F Major)

Also play:

etc.

Etude No. 11

GALLAY

LIP SLURS

sixth position _____ fifth position _____ fourth position _____

SIXTHS

Etude No. 12

MICHIELS

Andantino

p

mf

rit.

a tempo

p

Allegretto

mf

poco rit.

3

3

Tempo I

poco rit. *p*

VELOCITY STUDY

Also play:

A MINOR SCALE STUDY

Etude No. 13

SMALL

Allegretto

THIRDS

Also play:

etc.

Etude No. 14

Moderato

Etude No. 15

Moderato

LIP SLURS

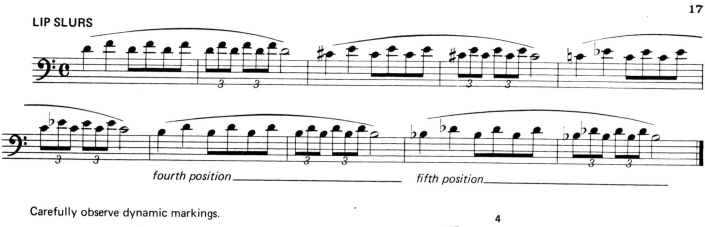

fourth position _____ *fifth position* _____

Carefully observe dynamic markings.

Etude No. 16

CONCONE

Moderato

dim. e rit.

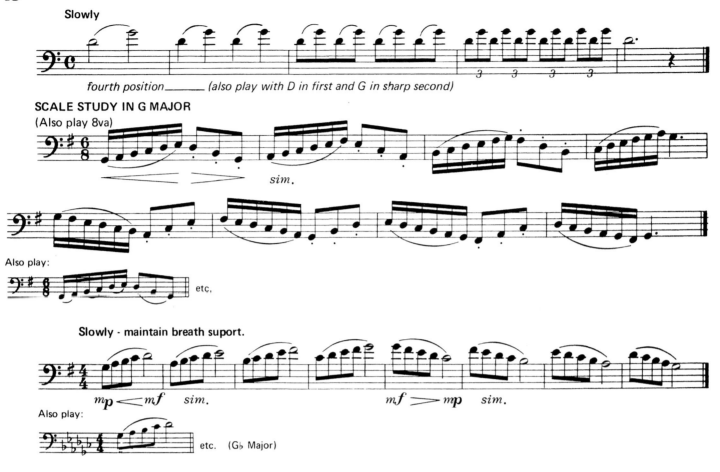

Slowly

fourth position_____ (also play with D in first and G in sharp second)

SCALE STUDY IN G MAJOR
(Also play 8va)

sim.

Also play:

etc,

Slowly - maintain breath suport.

mp < mf   sim.   mf > mp   sim.

Also play:

etc. (Gb Major)

Etude No. 17

Moderato

a tempo

INTERVALS

* Repeat previous two measures.

Etude No. 18

MICHIELS

Allegretto

STUDY IN G MINOR

Etude No. 19

KLOSE

LIP SLURS

fourth position _____

fifth position _____   *sixth position* _____

Bb MINOR SCALE STUDY

Etude No. 20

KOPPRASCH

Maestoso

LIP SLURS

fourth position _____ *fifth position* _____ *sixth position* _____

Play both ways:

Etude No. 21

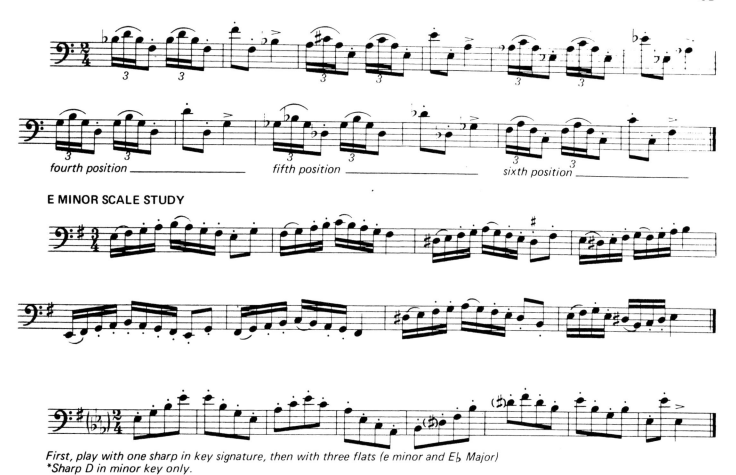

E MINOR SCALE STUDY

First, play with one sharp in key signature, then with three flats (e minor and E♭ Major)
*Sharp D in minor key only.

Etude No. 22

Polonaise

Etude No. 23

KOPPRASCH

Please refer to Part III, pages 39, 40 of the Method, "The Trombone Student" regarding the execution of Embellishments.

ARPEGGIOS

First, play with six flats in key signature – then one sharp (G♭ Major and G Major)

SCALE STUDY IN E♭ MINOR

Watch for tunes when the F is more conveniently played in 6th rather than 1st.

Etude No. 24

PAUDERT

CADENZA

When performing cadenzas, be very deliberate. Do not observe meter, but begin each section slowly increasing speed then ritard before each fermata. A smoothness and freeness of style is the keyword.

Etude No. 25

Etude No. 26

CADENZA

Etude No. 27

St. JACOME

CADENZA

Etude No. 28

SMALL

Grave

LIP SLURS

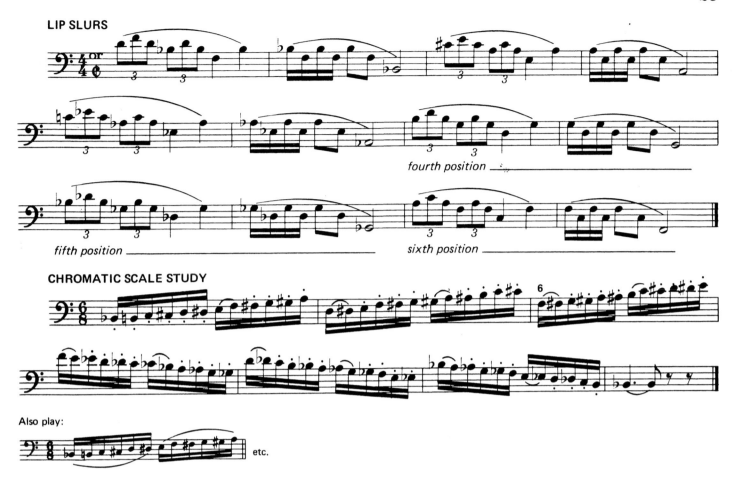

CHROMATIC SCALE STUDY

Also play:

etc.

Etude No. 29

TRIPLE TONGUING — Work for speed!

Etude No. 30

ARBAN

March tempo

DOUBLE TONGUING — Work for speed!

Etude No. 31

Allegro

ARBAN

TONGUING VARIATIONS (practice slowly and deliberately)

1. T T T T T etc.
2. K K K K K etc.

Note: Repeat the above using only the syllable Ka. Make it sound like single tonguing.

1. T K T K T etc.
2. K T K T K etc.

Note: Make each note sound alike. Equal emphasis should be given to each note.

Note: Practice the above exercise using the syllable Tu, then repeat using Ku.

1. T T K T T K T etc.
2. T K T K T K etc.

Note: Repeat the exercise using Ta, Ka, Ta, Ka, Ta, Ka. Make them uniform. They should sound like single tonguing.

Etude No. 32